EARTHLY DELIGHTS

PRINCETON SERIES OF CONTEMPORARY POETS
Susan Stewart, *series editor*

For other titles in the Princeton Series of Contemporary Poets see the end of this volume.

EARTHLY DELIGHTS

Poems

Troy Jollimore

PRINCETON UNIVERSITY PRESS
Princeton and Oxford

Published by Princeton University Press
41 William Street, Princeton, New Jersey 08540
6 Oxford Street, Woodstock, Oxfordshire OX20 1TR

press.princeton.edu

Library of Congress Cataloging-in-Publication Data

Names: Jollimore, Troy A., 1971– author.
Title: Earthly delights : poems / Troy Jollimore.
Description: First edition. | Princeton : Princeton University Press,
    [2021] | Series: Princeton series of contemporary poets
Identifiers: LCCN 2021003001 | ISBN 9780691218830 (hardcover) |
    ISBN 9780691218823 (paperback) | ISBN 9780691218847 (ebook)
Subjects: LCGFT: Poetry.
Classification: LCC PR9199.4.J658 E23 2021 | DDC 811/.6—dc23
LC record available at https://lccn.loc.gov/2021003001

British Library Cataloging-in-Publication Data is available

Editorial: Anne Savarese and James Collier
Production Editorial: Ellen Foos
Text Design: Pamela Schnitter
Jacket/Cover Design: Pamela Schnitter
Production: Erin Suydam
Publicity: Jodi Price and Amy Stewart
Copyeditor: Daniel Simon

Cover art: Joris Hoefnagel (1542–1600), *A Sloth*, 1561–1562.

This book has been composed in Adobe Garamond and Scala Sans

Printed on acid-free paper. ∞

Printed in the United States of America

10 9 8 7 6 5 4 3 2 1

Contents

LET THEM SEE THE IMAGES THAT
ARE DOOMED TO DISAPPEAR

THOUGH WE MAY AT TIMES ADMIRE
THE BEAUTY OF THEIR WEAPONS

SING THE STRING BENT SKYWARD

Ay, in the very temple of Delight
  Veil'd Melancholy has her sovran shrine
KEATS, "ODE ON MELANCHOLY"

For James Richardson

EARTHLY DELIGHTS

MUSE

Muse
wear me like clothing

fade into my skin
as I unfurl for you

like an oyster shell or
a work shirt bleached

by sunlight.
I've hung on the line for so long

here under the moon
to make this dark space

inside   where a song
can suffer and grow

Mouth, mouth
move against me

you will sing and then you will sing
then you will go

then I will sing
then I will sing

and then go

THE WHOLE SKY SPARKLING, ALL DIAMONDS

MARVELOUS THINGS WITHOUT NUMBER

Our duty is to see with the eyes of the gods.
STÉPHANE MALLARMÉ

After forty or so summers you kind of get
the idea: the slow deepening of the plum-blue dusk
that offers a backdrop for the stately silhouettes
of disconsolate, sentinel-like telephone poles;
the fading chorus of evening birdsong; the sharp hollow
pong of an aluminum bat making contact
with the ball somewhere off in the distance followed by
the joyful and at the same time somehow mildly
forlorn minor uproar of a clutch of children cheering;
eventless days at the beach, the scorched sand
stinging beneath your feet, the sand in
your clothes and your hair, a relentless ubiquitous
grit that remains undislodged after any
number of showers and shampooings; the familiar
dirt that collects underneath your fingernails
and your hair growing longer; careless
afternoons endured and discharged in the backyard
hammock or a languid folding chair by the lake,
reading Amy Clampitt, reading Rilke;
teenagers playing an eternal game
of Monopoly or Risk that might well be
the very same game they started last summer;
the same hummingbirds taking the same flight paths
back to the endless empty abundance
of the same backyard flowers and feeders . . .
Some friends are renewing their vows, they were married
a decade ago. Some friends are driving
up to one of the casinos on Friday
to hear a tribute band who have modeled themselves
after Led Zeppelin or Journey.

A friend who left for the East Coast two years
ago has flown back to Chico to take photos
of Mount Lassen exactly one hundred years after
its catastrophic eruption. For a while
it feels as if everything is a reenactment
of something that has already happened: even dumping
a skitter of Raisin Bran into a bowl
and then pouring milk over it, or sitting
on the porch or trying on sneakers takes on
the aura of a ritual. Are you trying
to deny time and change, to say that death
will have no authority here, or are you
celebrating the fact that everything is
in flux and ungraspable, or is the season
doing one or the other of these things for you?
Mornings glow like dreams, like memories, with
a radiance that has been lying latent
in the earth all night, you can do it again
(whatever *it* is) but you can't do it over:
the beautiful girl, kissed, can't be unkissed
(and who would want that anyway? But
you might), and so you repeat, repeat,
repeat, feeling rich with existence and time
and a kind of exhaustion you have learned to savor;
the end of Side B, after all, simply means
that you flip the record over and listen
to Side A again. And did you say that life
would always be this way, or were you told that
by someone in the past, and now hang on to that belief
in the face of what must be mounting but, for now,
still invisible evidence to the contrary?
Stay invisible, you say to it, stay, you whisper,
stay just as you are, just a little bit longer,
which is just another way of telling the story
you tell the children every night, how the birds
and the rivers remembered the songs even when

the people forgot, and how, when the people
regained the ability to remember,
they learned the songs again from the birds
and the rivers. The children's wide, trusting eyes
as you say this, as if what you said was, to use
that phrase we used to like to use, the gospel truth.
It's only a story, after all. You mean
no harm. No one means any harm. The world
is ancient, full of shades and spirits, not all of them
friendly, and we do with it what we can.

THAT LIFE

And did you think that life (that begins like a fire and consumes

and did you think that life (it unites you with beasts, you hold it in common

that life (given to you freely, but in what dream would you have pursued it

has been a series of standard answers (you put on your shoes and walked

to expected questions (to the city where they said the oracle was

and did you think that life (there is only one, despite the lies of the elders

has haunted you like a lost child (I mean wolves, yes, but also insects and clams

and are you being dramatic (I know you would deny it but you are dancing

or are you (a space is opening up on the inside, that's where the world is

parsing the words of the oracle (where the world goes, and yes you are dancing

and a space opens up on the inside of the world (yes that's where you go

and you go (and a space opens up, and the oracle falls into silence

like a child (there is only one, you fall silent, you fall silent then you go

to the city (where the fire and the beasts are, and the city falls into silence

and did you think that life? (and did you think *that*, life?

AT LIMANTOUR

At the water's edge you feel the mind of the planet
as if entering it from a different direction: the sharp
dry blades of the yellow and pale-green beach grasses,
the earth's cover versions of itself, clouds wisping
in the thin far-off blue, giving voice to a different
music, an alternative tone of thought,
and your own memories that for so long have perplexed you
fitting at last like jigsaw puzzle pieces
into a larger whole,
the entire interlocking superstructure something
you could not have guessed at but which now seems entirely
inevitable. What mad chance it is
to be, it is to be here, it is
to be an organism with a body that moves
and senses, gasping and singing,
and about to die if deprived for mere minutes
of the elements that sustain you. Despite
what you've said, the truth is that you do not mind
being loved, being seen in public places, being born
from the bodies of the predecessor animals, and giving
birth, in turn, to other animals,
the ones that will move away from you, to wander
and graze and soil the landscape. Your destiny
is here. If the stars are frozen on their surfaces,
not hot, as you have long suspected, nothing changes:
the crash of the breaking waves will roll down along
the beach to the place where you sit, and then past you,
remaining what it was, and the seeds that have gathered
together and given themselves your name
will not, in the end, refuse their mission. Gasping
and singing and sighing. Trembling in the wind,
trembling like the brittle shaking grasses. Call it dancing.

yes that's me
taking half a pill
because I cannot remember
whether I have already
taken one today

so this way
I know I'm wrong
but only a little wrong

and not in which direction

you have done this too
haven't you?
raise your hand if you have
no
the other one

raise your hand if you know
whereof I speak

raise your hand
if you have ever
asked your readers
to raise their hands
knowing they know
you can't see them

yes, you are of my tribe
of that we can now be certain

welcome, friend
here I am
living half a life
because I just can't remember

and this way
I know that I'm dead
but only a little

and not in which direction

welcome, friend
in the glass

at the bottom of the glass

bottomed

boat

are we in this together?
raise your hand if you are
raise your hand if I am
but you're not

raise your hand if
like me

you know whose ghost you want

to hover over this

POEM FOR GORD DOWNIE

You were always there, singing
from the back of the car
as if you were drunk back there dreaming and singing
while I drove aimlessly about the outskirts
of everybody's hometown
learning where the lovers go after dark
and practicing the names that had been rearranged
reassigned to the sacrosanct dark spaces
that remained underneath the crooked branches of the trees
and you were reconnoitering the impenetrable waters
of that vast silent sound
collectively known
as the collective Canadian unconscious
like someone searching for a drowned diver
or a slipped-off wedding ring.
A nation will watch me die, you sang
from back there, and I believed it the way you believe
something that somebody says in their sleep.
Fireworks by the side of the road, Northern Lights
and harbor lights perpetually enticing,
perpetually retreating, holding themselves
at a constant unbridgeable distance from my
ungovernable eyes. I flailed my way to
a first kiss as your face published itself
on every TV screen in every bar.
Last night I dreamed you were in my kitchen,
or else you are a sled dog on the snowy plain,
nuzzling the furry neck of Kurt Cobain.
Dancing to Schoenberg, drinking Schooner in Lunenburg.
And it was really you, wasn't it, who came paddling
past, really you whose psalms and sonics
sang the stoic poles together? I think now that maybe
we were not a nation until we watched you

sing and die. O Gord, I lift this last round
to the sprawling sound of the gravid growlings
you brought up from those dark waters
and the verses you engraved on the vast white wall
of unmusic that we face but cannot force ourselves to face.
Listen now, that wail from the West's waste-effaced margins.
Listen now, these foreign shores, these fallen final invitations.
Listen now, this ceaseless silence you have signed and left behind you.

EARLY MORNING, UPPER BIDWELL PARK

The world drawn like a bowstring

        as if to test the returned warrior

and the suitors failing in the room
decorated by Penelope's latest unweavings

When God made the world he did it like this

        world-making in the daytime
        world-undoing at night

And it has occurred to me that we might be living

        in one of the undoings

*

Later she told a lie about their bed

        another test
        for the returned wanderer

the man who claimed to have spent
so many nights there

        and so many nights away

to have had so many dreams there
a pair of love-craft traveling side by side

        soft points of contact
        soft points of departure
        soft points of approximate presence

kiss, coo, murmur, softly shift

*

    and then, the ten-year absence

during which news was slow to arrive if it
arrived at all

        the night twice as long
        the bed twice as cold

*

If I were to make a world
not beginning *ex nihilo* but with what there is

I think there would be more unmaking than making
not that I would undo

the marvelous spatuletail hummingbird,
the right whale, the sunrise, butter-and-eggs,
the green-blooded skink, the Blanding's turtle

these I would let be
but we agree
there are other phenomena
of more recent, more human origin.

        things put together by bodies

        with eyes and hands like mine.

*

You remember how light our bodies were
when we lifted them into the trees?
How pure the water and the song.
And the unknown sources of water and song.

The little blue butterfly I've been watching

       all this time
       has finally settled

on the rock like a whisper, folding its wings
like a hand someone has decided not to play.

       Its shut-up wings, like the sails of a tiny, delicate boat, are pale.

So much more colorful, for whatever reason,
when it's in the air.

UNEARNED SEASON

the sun still beneath

the horizon and already

a bird at the feeder

a bee at the flower

and a mosquito sent

but by whom?

to trouble me

out of some unrelenting slumber

another summer

unearned season

universe's origin

receding before

our attempts to understand

and gearing up again

as if to regenerate

necessary conditions

for nightfall

they used to sell oranges in

the theater to cover

the scent of human bodies

that social, neighborly

stench, though your own

or, if not that, your lover's

is perhaps pleasing

tell me, is anything

human

alien,

truly?

a sip

of whiskey counts

as the night

before's

and so

you say to yourself

of morning

now and your brain

strawberries

to sing and to do

to sing and aspire to do

to do

no harm done

necessary conditions

the sun just coming up

seized by the odor of

sing and take aim

to sing and to sing and take aim

for once, today,

no harm

ANDRÉ GREGORY SAID

But there is two hard things; that is, to bring the moonlight into a
chamber; for, you know, Pyramus and Thisby meet by moonlight.
A MIDSUMMER NIGHT'S DREAM

André Gregory said
that he wanted to put
a human head
in a play. From a corpse,
that is to say,
as a way
of making the audience feel
that this was *real:*
lives being lived out
and brought to an end
on this very stage,
which all the world's a,
as we know,
not merely set
and struck
to present
a passing show.
To have us
pass it around,
fresh death in our hands,
to see if we
can withstand
an art that cleaves
so tightly to
things as they are,
if one can stand
another skull
so near one's own,
one on, one off,

one live, one not,
one more performance
of the plot
(if one can withstand
its demands) that's never
quite the same
one night to the next
so there is no question
of *owning*, but only
of being present,
or rather, of having
been, and the having been
having been followed
by a quick exit
pursued by a fill-in-the-
blank, each actor's
pursuer uniquely
his, each audience
member dismembered
in her own manner,
death by silence, death
by moonlight,
death by monologue,
what doesn't kill you
kills another,
what doesn't kill you
makes you stronger,
what doesn't kill you
now kills you
tomorrow, takes just
that much longer.

SCREENSHOTS: *VANYA ON 42ND STREET*

The temperature of the water being
indiscernible from that of the air

so that you can't tell when you have slipped in
and when you are walking about on dry land

or whether the man before you is really
napping, exhausted by the demands

of his acting career, or playing a man
who is napping, exhausted by the demands

of managing a nineteenth-century estate
in agrarian Russia, envisioned by Chekhov,

re-envisioned by a man last seen
in an upscale New York restaurant, having dinner

with a vaguely familiar, somewhat shorter man,
both of them burdened with names and stories

that are theirs and also are not theirs,
both of them performing, both transforming

harshness into loveliness, graffiti-gray day
into vibrant, pulsing, luminous night,

unable to tell, perhaps, when they slip
into or back out of their roles

in this slow-collapsing, this decomposing,
this disappearing theater.

To have no screen between this part he played
and him he played it for.

Blue pigment paints mountains and rivers.
A rice cake is painted with powdered rice.

Perhaps in the end, we will find a place,
onstage or off, where we can rest.

We shall see the angels. We shall see
the whole sky sparkling, all diamonds.

SCREENSHOTS: *NOSTALGHIA*

And in conclusion, isn't that just what our life is all about,
to get across the empty pool before the candle flickers out?

Because order matters: breakfast, then lunch,
then dinner, dessert following the main course;
the orgasm, yes, but the foreplay before;
old age, yes, but first youth:
Dante's *Divine Comedy* only considered
a "comedy" in so far as it ends
in Paradise, having first given us
a grand tour of the Inferno and then
Purgatory, as methodical if not
quite so easy as A, B, C;
so that, when we look at Bosch's *Garden*
of Earthly Delights, it matters whether
we read it, as readers of English will tend to,
from left to right, beginning in Paradise,
where Dante's masterpiece ends,
then passing through that ebullient garden
bursting with the planet's abundance of pleasures
on the way to that culminating, grotesque,
and, one assumes, irrevocable final
destination, the grim fate that we, in Dante,
climb out of—we, that is, the readers,
the viewers, the detached, impartial observers,
carrying the passports that permit us safe passage
into and out of these unearthly zones,
and not, by any means, the internees,
those who have been granted, against their will
and without their asking (though Dante's Virgil
would have disagreed, insisting that they did,
in effect, ask for this, that they did indeed will it)
permanent residence status—or whether,
in fact, we read it in some other way,
as, for example, presenting these
three states of being as being suspended

before us all at once, as if,
at any moment, we might slip partially
or even completely into any one of them,
or, for that matter, as if at any moment,
an elemental intrusion from hell or paradise
might erupt, without warning, into our lives—
so that the story is not a tale of causation
(sin leads to hell, light to darkness, delight
to damnation) but rather a manner of grasping
the complexity of our existence, how things
that are opposite, if they do not attract,
at the very least coexist, taking place
in one and the same moment, the disparate
constituents of human life that do not,
as one might have expected, when brought into contact,
annihilate one another, but instead,
by the very force of their contrast, heighten
and strengthen each other. What, other than evil,
could make virtue shine so bright? What, other than
purity and naïve hope, could entice
corruption and despair into bursting forth
to appear so nakedly as what they are?

Because order matters, yes; but our lives
are not orderly. And art, precisely
because it is, feels at times like a mere
detached imitation, yet can also feel
as if it were more like life than life
itself. Which is why, one assumes, we are drawn,
again and again, to the place where the picture
hangs, to stand in its presence, as if
it were only in those moments that we lived.

But we come from elsewhere, and we go elsewhere
when we are done with our looking. That they
are *earthly* delights, indeed, reminds us

that Dante's *Commedia*, too, begins
not in hell but on earth: that famous dark wood,
not a garden of delights, not at all, but a kind
of garden nevertheless, and that
an arrival in Paradise might well take
the form, as in that remarkable final
shot of Tarkovsky's *Solaris*, of
a return to Earth, a real Earth or
a reconstructed Earth, an imagined
garden or a painted garden, or simply
the garden where you were born. The leafy
globe, perhaps, that we see when the triptych
is closed. It is the earth that is ours,
and Dante's cosmic love, though it moves
the stars that track their paths through their skies,
is a leafy thing, a fleshly thing,
a thing of the soil, a thing that demands
to be lived out on this surface, on the face
of this terrestrial sphere, this local
unheavenly orb, this, our planet,
our neighborhood, if, that is
to say, it is to be lived at all.

THE REPUBLIC FORGETS

A TOAST

(*"Salut," Stéphane Mallarmé, 1893*)

It's nothing, spume-poem, pure froth
Names nothing, names only this vessel
In some faraway sea drowns a passel
Of muse-mermaids, ass-over-teakettle

So, my various friends, we traverse
These waters—I astern and on course,
You the lush avant-garde, cleaving asunder
The onrushing flood-tide of winters and thunder

A drunk spell, so lovely, inspires me—
Though the deck's pitching, I'm without fear—
To stand and toast what we hold dear:

Solitude, rock-reef, or star
Whatever it is that calls forth
The salute of our bright blank sail-cloth.

1

The ground swells. The tidal bore moans. The American
people have spoken. *I think they just said*
something, Paul Newman murmurs, his ears
detecting a far-off rumble in Aleppo.
Free Chelsea Clinton. Free stay at the Chelsea
Hotel. Free Taryn Manning. Free bonus
disk of special features. One hundred
percent media saturation, one hundred
percent virtual digital market penetration!
American democracy at rock-bottom fire-sale
prices! You've never seen a deal like this!
Today only, every purchase of a canister
of carcinogens saves one ten-thousandth of a duck!
Me me me me mimes the Meme in Chief
all day and all night, as his constituency
drifts into the most unimpeachable of slumbers.
Zero percent disinterest for forty-eight
months. This offer is unforgivable.
Free the Chicago Seven for the first fifty
customers enrolling in our Special Friends plan,
which offers unlimited calls to everyone
who votes the same way as you. Free Kindle
Jenner. This posse grabs back. It is said
the frog does not think to jump out of the water
as the water gets hotter. The American people
are joking. We are forced to assume. Void where
uninhibited, limit of one
beheading per customer. Maybe my brand
could go to bed with your brand?

They're all dead now, who says a vote makes no difference?
Our amazing new product lightens dark skin,
making police interactions more comfortable and less frequent!

2

Meanwhile, at Walden Pond, Henry Thoreau
clicks *like* on the 'Pristine Wilderness' page.

3

I fled the agents and their swag
to the Entitled Status of Miracle.
Please pardon our disappearance.
We are open during destruction.

4

Protect your constitutional rights!
with our Extended Warranty Plan,
just nine ninety-nine ninety-nine per month
with credit approval. And while you're at it,
try our fat-free fat and fat-free free-range chicken.
The American people are stricken.
The gated communities cry, *Stop breathing
our air!* I can see their point, I sym-
pathize, choke, choke. Like you, Robert Lowell,
I'm also waiting for that blessed bubble to break.
Like you, Robert Lowell, I also think
this could use a little more salt.
Free your mind and how many corpses will follow?
Freedom isn't free.
But this week only, it's half off.

Halfway through my annual active-shooter training,
I found myself lost, as if in a dark wood,
imagining gunfire's refrain. Refraining

from any noise that might betray me, that could,
had the man in our building been an actual intruder,
not an actor in camo, be fatal, I stood

and waited (for these serve as well). My computer
soft-slumbered in SLEEP mode through dreams of math.
Halfway through our annual required active-shooter

training, I found myself wondering what path
had led to this place. Had some limit expired?
Had we slept through gunfire's shocked refrain? Only death,

not mere sleep—o, surely not sleep!—could inspire
such bureaucratized chaos. The death of the spirit,
collapse of old forms. Halfway through my required

active-shooter training I imagine I can hear it,
the retort and refrain of gunfire. Restraining
myself from running after, from trying to get near it,

I shelter in place, soft-recite the old story
of competent adults in charge, maintaining
that all's well, all ends well. Halfway through our mandatory

annual supervised active-shooter training,
I ask how we ended up here, our hopes waning,
huddled in our dark offices, silent, ears straining

for far-off shots, emblems of immortal danger.
My body as still as a bullet in a chamber.
Halfway through our annual active-shooter training
the gunfire chorus at last stops refraining.

1

To take seriously the proposition that disappearance is the normal order of things.

2

Gene and I decided to go to the movies. Gene had a rough time around people because of how his face worked. When he was sad his face registered joy. When he liked someone his face registered fear. But he liked watching movies, where he could see but not be seen. But when we got to what we thought was the right address we found that the movie theater had been replaced by a baseball stadium which had in turn been replaced by a labyrinthine complex of self-storage rental units. And the city itself, the beautiful city that used to surround the movie theater, had been replaced by a military research facility which had in turn been replaced by desert. It was too late to go home, and fortunately there were a few other people there as confused as we were, who let us join their camp and shared their water with us while we considered what to do next.

3

Silence and residue of waters, radio waves, ungrounded ground.
At the end of the ceremony nothing had been bought, but so much,
   so much had been sold.

4

To wake up in the middle of a dream without the dream
ending, to wonder how this could be unless it were someone
else's dream, or not a dream at all, but rather
a pageant of sorts, a gratuitous gift. *Love is theater,*

she said, and you thought this was nothing, just a standard
part of the seduction, but later, in the room you borrowed
to make love to her, you felt, dimly, the presence
of an audience, and then you noticed that the actor
assigned to play her part had been switched
with another.

5

And then the corporation announced that it was about to initiate a
new program called Amazon Preemptive Delivery, in which as soon as
you mentioned or even thought about a product a drone would be
dispatched to deliver it to you, and the charges automatically deducted
from your account. Average delivery time would be two and a half
minutes, meaning that your bright new purchase would often have
arrived before you were even aware that you wanted it.

6

The man who made the announcement was wearing an Italian
suit that fit his body the way a field of wildflowers
fits a hillside meadow and would respond to objections
from various members of the assembly
by sighing and saying to the ceiling, "There are always,
in every era, those whose primary desire
is to impede the path of progress."

7

A thing on a stage is perceived by so many eyes at once
it can practically disappear beneath the weight of all that seeing.

8

Which explains, perhaps, the dream of being an actor.

9

No fact of the matter, in our view, as to whether
an attraction existed that brought these two figures into orbit
around each other or some bored divinity
had decided to manipulate the game, the flow
of things, merely self-entertaining with the nearest-
to-hand playthings he could manage to find,
which happened, on this occasion, to be human.
At any rate, their habit was to meet at noon
in the lobby of the Prudential Building. And what
is a building, after all, but a larger, more durable
set of clothes that many people can wear
all at once? And what is a smile, but a way
of speaking without speaking? And what is lovemaking
but a way of saying to one's surroundings,
I, too, belong among the items that have been placed here?

10

Silence and residue of waters, radio waves, ungrounded ground.
At the end of the ceremony nothing had changed hands, but our
    hands had been somehow changed.
It was our hands themselves that confronted us now, fresh-born,
    unrecognized, strange.

ZAPRUDER FILM BLOOPER REEL

Till some retrieveless Night
Our Vigilance at waste
The Garden gets the only shot
That never could be traced.
EMILY DICKINSON

What like a bullet can undeceive!
HERMAN MELVILLE

The shooter forgets to take the shot.
The president forgets to fall.
The pink sleeve of Jackie's suit gets caught
in the door. The man on the grassy knoll

neglects to reload. He misses the shot.
The man on the sixth floor neglects to reload.
He misses the shot. Jackie's sleeve gets caught.
The president whispers to her in code.

The crowd of bystanders, primed for a show,
forgets to be shocked. The president falls
so gorgeously they erupt into
spontaneous, heartfelt applause.

The lighting is wrong. Jackie misses her mark.
The president stumbles over his lines.
We lose the light. The image goes dark.
The rifle jams. The Director resigns

himself to another take. The man
pauses to reload on the grassy knoll.
This country, he says. *They can put a man*
on the moon, but you can't make him drink. The role

of the second shooter will now be played
by a stand-in whose name everyone forgot.
He hits his mark. His image fades.
The shooter forgets to make the shot.

The A.D. calls *Cut!* The Director calls *Action!*
Blood and flesh light up the screen.
The image for this week's Write Your Own Caption
Contest is frame number three thirteen.

The camera jams. It's a beautiful shot.
He watches it pass from the grassy knoll.
Jackie nails her lines. Her image is caught.
The Republic forgets, or does not, not to fall.

SCREENSHOTS: *ETERNAL SUNSHINE OF THE SPOTLESS MIND*

Eternal sunshine of the spotless mind.
That's Pope. And tell me, who remembers Pope?
The sky grows dark. The books go blank. Remind-
ers of our former lives, regrets, and hopes

are zapped into the void, the great lacuna,
as, grain by grain, the sand is washed away.
("It's just a bunch of tiny rocks," some say.)
Ignorance is bliss, they murmur—*but*—no sooner

have we been brought to see it as a boon,
unlocking our brains to those detail-scrubbers,
than we begin to moan a different tune:
I don't want this . . . But where is our dream lover

who'll meet us at Montauk, as per the plot?
A girl for getting, by a girl forgot . . .

This is *No Country for Old Men.* The young
Llewellyn Moss, a Texan born and bred,
happens upon a cash-cache and some dead
hombres. He'll join those corpses before long,

dispatched not by a captive-bolt stun gun
to his serenely confident forehead,
as some folks, like our good friend Sheriff Ed
Tom, had predicted—no, our hero's done

in off-screen by some nameless killer. Death,
in this rough country, is anonymous
and indiscriminate, indifferent as

the tossed coin that determines your last breath,
or the formula that graphs the curved flight plan
of a bag of cash tossed into no-man's-land.

SCREENSHOTS: *THE TALENTED MR. RIPLEY*

How bad is my pain, she asks him,
on a scale of one to ten?

It's a zero, he says. *A flat zero.*
Hell, I just don't feel it at all.

NEXT LIFE

For my next life
I'll need a volunteer from the audience.
Something in a 36 Long would be nice.
Something in an endless line
of sleek black cars
with a coffee bar in back
and exhaust that tickles the nostrils
like sweet juniper trees in the first cool hour of evening.
Someone who will stand erect
and unashamed
before the committee
and not name names.
Something in a self-propelled
Auto-Tune disaster
that would drive anyone's parents
off the deep end.
After so many years
you'd think we'd understand
the complex second stage
of the secret handshake,
or know where to get
a good sandwich in these parts,
or at least know enough
not to risk the lives
of all sixty-three members of the submarine crew
by diving to the bottom
of the ocean in search
of a bell the captain heard,
or thought he heard,
in a dream
when he was only seven years old.

ALL THE MYSTERIES

Darkness, from which all mysteries arise. The darkness between the legs, the darkness behind the eyes. What if, what if we did not weep and wail when we were born or died, but only smiled? Like everyone, I have known the darkness of the cities by the ocean, I have walked into the darkness that separates the small settlements that punctuate the plain. Now there is no darkness but only light, light everywhere, light always, ceaselessly produced and pumped into the insatiable empty world, the limitless dark world our vision can no longer detect or contain.

After all these years we still occupy white buildings beside gray oceans. Tall buildings constructed by people who came before us, who carried into the world, who carried out, their own ideas. Their ideas of shelter and order, their visions of contentment and peace. People who tried to free us by leaving us structures that, in the intervening time, have grown to resemble cages. Their ghosts, their remnants, go marching day and night, unresting, up and down the stairs. We, the living, take the elevators in order to avoid them. We sit inside the offices we have claimed and put our names on, in these buildings we have inherited and taken as our own, and we spread out the plans on the flat surfaces of the desks where others used to sit, where other plans were spread out by other hands, other pencils lodged behind other ears. Planning how we will take the desks apart, and then the buildings after. And then the streets, and then the plazas, and then, after that, the cities themselves.

Making plans to disassemble all the things our predecessors put together.

And all the while we hear them in the stairways, walking up, walking down.

And all the while, behind us, behind all the visible things, the stars, the silent and unseen stars that are such a terror to us, and to each other, and to anyone with eyes to see.

THE POEM YOU WILL NOT LIVE TO WRITE

The poem you will not live to write—
the poem you would have written if only
you'd had one more month, one more day, one more hour—
is a killer. A no-holds-barred, balls-out
masterpiece, the one where you put it all
together, everything you learned, everything
you suffered, all the bits of being human
you spent your life gathering up. It's the poem
you have been waiting for all your life.

The poem you will not live to write—
the next poem you would have written after
the last poem you will write, which is,
it must be said, a perfectly decent,
unexceptionable, un-
exceptional poem, the sort of poem
you would have read in some magazine
or other had someone else been the author,
or made it through the first half, anyway,
and then maybe turned to the theater
reviews or the gossip column or else
just put the whole tiresome issue aside—
is, let's just admit it, a knockout.

There's no avoiding the fact.
The poem you will not live to write
is the one that would make the grocer's daughter
come back to you, it's the poem you'd wear
like a pair of expensive stolen shoes
to a wedding you weren't invited to,
it's the one that waits for you in the dark,

unseen in the underbrush just outside
the campfire's zone of protected light,
with nothing but an uninhibited passionate
kiss and your death on its mind.

That sound that sometimes enters the world
as thunder, at others as the boisterous crashing
of waves. That rustling in the bushes

that designates either the wind or the twitching
of unseen lurkers. That smile from the bride
at the altar, expressing nothing or else

confessing *I wish it were not him but you.*
That siren's wail telling you *this is a test,*
this is only a test, if it isn't screaming

you and everyone here are about
to die an unpleasant and very newsworthy
death. That kiss that translates as *your life*

has just ended but possibly means *your life*
is only beginning. That buzzing that says
you are getting old and your hearing is going,

unless, of course, a swarm of bees
is nearby. That look from a beautiful stranger
that means *keep your distance* or maybe it means

come closer, I get off at eight, I have
a room on the third floor, here is the key.
That little red splotch on the skin that signifies

nothing at all, unless it's a sign
that you should perhaps get it checked, though of course
it's already so late that getting it checked

will not save you. That sweet post-sunset moment
of melancholy that's there to remind you
that this life, your only life, is not really

yours, that you have assumed it like
a disguise, that you should have done what you really
wanted to do—trained as a chef,

a guitarist, traveled the world as a broke
and itinerant vagabond—and means,
as well, that on such evenings any

existence you might have pursued would have felt
like something assigned or stolen, that time flows
in one direction only, that now

it takes three drinks to make the music
sound the way it's supposed to sound,
that the taste of the air on late summer evenings

is always a little bit bitter, always
a little bit tinged with regret, that this is
your language, your city, and no one but you

can speak it, and no one but you can save it.

LET THEM SEE THE IMAGES
THAT ARE DOOMED TO
DISAPPEAR

SCREENSHOTS: *BEING JOHN MALKOVICH*

Being John Malkovich, John Malkovich
was pretty much the inevitable choice
to play the character 'John Malkovich.'
Who else could imitate that wheedling voice,

who else could skew his odd expressions so?
As the old saying has it, *Be yourself,*
who else is better qualified? But know,
the very question that the film itself

forces us to confront is, who *am* I
when someone else lives through me? Are we holes,
mere absences, possessed and occupied

by one of a parade of passing souls
that grip the reins and take us for a ride?
Malkovich is Malkovich. But so am I.

SCREENSHOTS: *BOOGIE NIGHTS*

Because it's not the size of the camera,
it's how long you can hold the shot.

SCREENSHOTS: *COCKSUCKER BLUES*

If there were dreams to sell,
what would you buy?
THOMAS LOVELL BEDDOES, "DREAM-PEDLARY"

The lyric's
first-person
is haunted

by the growl
of impending
regret:

you might
sometimes get
what you wanted

but you can't
always want
what you get

AMERICAN BEAUTY

*As Americans, we are citizens of a large, secular, commercial democracy; we are
relentlessly borne forth on the flux of historical change, routinely flung laterally by
the exigencies of dreams and commerce.*
DAVE HICKEY, "AMERICAN BEAUTY"

When the Senator Theatre closed in 1999 in Chico, California,
the last film to be shown was *American Beauty*, and so I went, for the last
    screening.
I went to take in the last images, to feel the last light, to be a part
of the end of something, to be, I suppose, a kind of witness, and to be a part
of that crowd of others who also felt that they wanted or needed to go,
to go to the movies for whatever reason it is that humans go to the movies—
because we are all scopophiliacs, perhaps; because we all get lonely;
because we think that the only way we can touch the people around us
is to share some spectacle with them, to feel the same feeling, to see the same
    sight,
to think the same thought, to be moved all in the same direction like a school
    of fish
or a flock of sparrows shot like a host of arrows from some unearthly bow,
swooping and twisting in unison, pouring through itself like a waterfall,
to be moved by an unforgettable image or a perfectly delivered line of
    dialogue,
or the music, some melody that seems to embody sadness itself,
that teeters and balances on the edge of being manipulative and then
    somehow
stops exactly on its mark and dances there. So that, when Lester Burnham
dies (oh, *spoiler alert,* by the way—but not really, since, after all, he himself
tells us in the first few minutes of the film that he's going to die at the end)
it is a death we can share, a loss we can call our own, each of us imagining
our own body in that spot, in that shot, the shot that shows his slumped
    corpse, the one that follows
the shot that kills him, imagining our own head on the table, our own blood
freshly freed and flowing, as that creepy, fascinated kid looks on, finding
    beauty

in everything, even the horrible, as he has been trained, as an American, to do.
(For even the corpse, as Emerson says, possesses its own beauty.)
We lost Lester Burnham that night, and ourselves, and then we lost the
    Senator.
No more movies. No more projected light. No more sitting with strangers in
    the dark.

*

What I'm trying to say is, over ninety percent of American films that were
    made
prior to 1929, and half of American sound films made before 1950,
no longer exist. The original ending of Orson Welles's *The Magnificent
    Ambersons*,
which some have said was, in its original form, better than *Citizen Kane,*
no longer exists. Some studio executive dumped it while Welles was out of
    the country.
Into the ocean with all that footage, sunk like a trireme, to be silently
corroded by salt water over the decades to come. What I'm trying to do is sing
the song of all the screens we will never sit in front of, all the images
that once composed themselves before human eyes and that might have
    moved us, you
and I, together, in the same direction, dancing together without moving,
wandering together, perhaps—for as Scottie says to Madeleine in *Vertigo*,
Only one is a wanderer, two together are always going somewhere—
but will never have the chance to do that, because time, as it does—it is,
    after all,
the very nature of time—got to them first and has taken them away.

*

Mothers of America,
I second Frank O'Hara's sentiment.
Let your kids go to the goddamn movies!
In fact, don't just let them go,
make them go.

Otherwise they will develop relationships
with their parents
(that is to say, you)
that are far too close
to not be unhealthy,
and they will stay indoors
and watch movies on their iPhones,
and will never understand,
because you never made them go
to the theater to be awed and overwhelmed,
that watching a movie on an iPhone
is like licking a picture of a cake,
it's like making love through a telescope,
because it is in the nature of things
that the movies should be larger
than us,
not that we should be larger than them.

Let them see the images
that are doomed to disappear,
the ones that time will take away.
The images those
who are yet to come
and inhabit this planet
will speculate about
and try to imagine
but will never get to see.

Also, theater attendance
is at its lowest level
since 1992,
and you aren't helping.

*

The growth of a large business is merely survival of the fittest. The American Beauty rose can be produced in the splendor and fragrance which brings cheer to its beholder only by sacrificing the early buds which grow around it. This is not an evil tendency in business. It is merely the working out of a law of nature and a law of God.

JOHN D. ROCKEFELLER JR.

*

Or else we think it's the people up on the screen that we are touching,
those vast figures made of light, who seem not only more vibrant but
    somehow
more real than these small poorly-lit three-dimensional bodies, these shuffling
    shambles that carry,
buried deep inside them, the seeds of death; delusional thinking, it goes,
perhaps, without saying, as there is after all nothing to touch up there, you
    might
as well try to touch a sunset or a rainbow. No, if we are going to touch,
to take comfort in each other, to feel the warmth of the spirit as it manifests
in the flesh, it must be the flesh of the person sitting in the seat beside you
in the darkened theater, or perhaps the person sitting two rows back,
who you have yet to meet, but who you noticed, perhaps, on the way inside,
in the ticket line, or who, perhaps, noticed you, and who you will, it's possible,
bump serendipitously into out in the lobby after the show,
and go on to strike up a conversation about what you have just seen,
a conversation that might go who knows where? or perhaps you came
tonight with someone who you met, in just this way, years ago? There is a
    bond
that forms between two people when they see, in one moment, as if they
    shared
a single pair of eyes, and saw the world as one, the same beauty.

I myself feel a little hesitant about the idea of appealing to,
or of stating, in anything that might seem to resemble precise or concrete
    terms,
the laws of nature, let alone, for heaven's sake, the laws of God.

But then, I'm no Rockefeller.

And it is hard to think that Alan Ball, when he wrote *American Beauty*,
did not have this precise passage of Rockefeller's in mind.
For isn't this what Lester Burnham is doing, precisely, indeed, what he is doing,
trying to bring himself cheer, attempting to explode, in midlife, into splendor
(*American Splendor*—now there's an interesting film—but that's another story)
at the cost of sacrificing the early buds that are growing around him?

And if one of those early buds, the one that happens to have captured his
    attention,
should happen to be, not a flower, literally, but rather, a teenaged girl,
some young person, only just now discovering for herself her own body's
    capacity for joy—

must he hold himself back, on that account?
Does that really make a difference?

It is not an evil tendency, many say.
It is only a law of nature.

*

The ancient Greeks called the world κόσμος *beauty. Such is the constitution of all
things, or such the plastic power of the human eye, that the primary forms, as the
sky, the mountain, the tree, the animal, give us a delight in and for themselves; a
pleasure arising from outline, color, motion, and grouping. This seems partly owing
to the eye itself. The eye is the best of artists. By the mutual action of its structure
and of the laws of light, perspective is produced, which integrates every mass of
objects, of what character soever, into a well colored and shaded globe, so that where
the particular objects are mean and unaffecting, the landscape which they compose,
is round and symmetrical. And as the eye is the best composer, so light is the first of
painters. There is no object so foul that intense light will not make beautiful. And
the stimulus it affords to the sense, and a sort of infinitude which it hath, like space
and time, make all matter gay. Even the corpse has its own beauty.*
    RALPH WALDO EMERSON, *Nature*

*

(And you have met his brothers
skulking in the bushes
with their video-recorders.)

*

And must we clutter this verse
with the news
of what the star of the film has been up to

lately? O muse,
the gnarled, stunted forms you sing through
are not what you deserve.

*

There are, it should be mentioned, two other films called *American Beauty*,
    both lost.
One from 1916, a drama directed by William Desmond Taylor, starring
    Myrtle Stedman
and Elliott Dexter. The screenplay is by Julia Crawford Ivers, whose other
    credits include
The White Flower (she had a thing for flowers, perhaps), *Sacred and Profane
    Love*,
and *Married Flirts*. The plot, according to the Internet Movie Database,
concerns the daughter of a wealthy couple who is believed to be lost at sea,
who somehow comes into the care, and is raised by, a poverty-stricken family.
I wonder what John D. Rockefeller Jr. would have made of that.

The other lost *American Beauty*, which dates from 1927
and was directed by Richard Wallace, was based on a story by Wallace Irwin
and starred Billie Dove as Millicent Howard, a beautiful young woman
who makes it appear, through a variety of creative ruses, that she comes from
    money

though in fact she has none, as a way of trying to attract, or, as people used
    to say,
to "land," a wealthy husband. One begins to sense a theme,
class mobility, success in the classic American mode, the question of how
    one gets
to the top from the bottom, and how a quick sudden fall can take you back
    down.
The question of how much of it concerns appearance, how one is perceived,
speaking right and dressing correctly, dining on the proper things.
The question of chance, the role it plays in lifting and lowering us.
The question of whether there isn't some better arrangement we might have
    made of things.

The name of the man that Millicent Howard sets her sights on, by the way,
is Archibald Claverhouse. People don't have names like that anymore.

*

I'm not saying, incidentally,
that we should tell the kids
the movies are *good* for them.

Like kale,
or flu shots,
or retirement accounts.

Good god, no.

Let's tell them, in fact,
that the movies are positively
bad for them.

Because, first of all,
there's some truth to that.

And because, secondly,
they understand better
than the rest of us, sometimes,
that getting too much of what's good for you
is not always good for you.

*

There is, too, the El Rey, a few streets away from the Senator, on Second Street,
which opened in 1906. Its first show, a set of films titled "Whitney's
Celebrated Life Motion Pictures," included *The Fire Bug*, *Great Mine Disaster*,
and *Scenes of the Russian Revolution*. Advertisements for the show
promised that attendees would experience "Positively
No Flicker or Vibration." At that time it was known as The Majestic,
later rechristened The National, then The American, and finally, the El Rey.

It was mostly shut down in 2005. I saw *The Man Who Wasn't There*
in that theater, and *Sideways*, which was the last first-run film to be shown
in that place before it closed, and I have, at least twice, dreamed about being
inside, with its beautiful art deco mural of yellow fairies and flowers,
the entire fantastical scene set against a deep-blue background.

If there were dreams to sell—but would you? and to sell for what?
I'll let you be in my, if I can dream, if you—it's alright, this
Is all a dream we—what did you— a dream—we dreamed—we told you
    what to—

*

In 1908, on Christmas Eve, George McClellan, mayor of New York City,
ordered that hundreds of motion picture theaters in that city be closed.
He had, he told the public, witnessed for himself the unsafe conditions
the theaters manifested, not to speak (though speak he did, with relish)
of the outrageous, immoral behavior the picture shows encouraged.
He had found, he said, emergency exits that did not open,
exits that led to forty-foot drops, exits that led the unwary

directly into Turkish baths. *Turkish baths!* Supporting his decision,
the Reverend Evers, chaplain of City Prison, told reporters, "I was amazed
by the exhibitions I saw for the benefit of the little boys
and girls of our city. The most suggestive, the most enticing actions
which appeal only to the lower and most evil passions in men and women
were thrown upon the screen for small boys and girls to look upon.
I was indeed saddened by this open exhibition of depravity."

Picking up the charge, Vincent Pisarro, the chief investigator for
the Society for the Prevention of Cruelty to Children, identified movie
    theaters
as locations where young boys were enticed into criminal lives—trained as
    pickpockets—
and where young girls sold their innocence. "The darkness of the auditorium
    during
the exhibitions," he opined, encouraged seduction, providing ample
opportunity for "'puppy love' affairs." And as if that weren't damning enough,
other clergy observed that the movie industry was, in actuality,
"a Jewish syndicate furnishing indecencies for the city."

*

The eye is the best of artists,
though the hand, the hand does what it can.

The Invisible Hand called in sick today.
It's getting a manicure.

The Invisible Hand is in the corner
giving us all the finger.

An invisible finger. Huh.
Well, would you look at that.

Doesn't look like much from here.
Not even the most intense light

in the universe would make *that* look like
anything at all.

*

What I'm trying to say is that beautiful things have a way of making us
    anxious.
What I'm trying to say is that no one knows what we might get up to in the
    dark,
which is perhaps why we've tried so hard to blanket our planet in light,

as if that would make it beautiful. As if the planet were unclean.
What I'm trying to say is that caring for things, taking care of them,
    preserving them,
is, perhaps, not our forte. By 'our,' I mean to refer to us, this race

of rampant overdeveloped monkeys that has spread all over the planet,
and that you and I, my friend, are card-carrying members of.
What I'm trying to say is, eighteen of Euripides' plays have come down to us

(he wrote over ninety), a mere seven by Aeschylus (sources say he too wrote
    ninety),
and seven, again, by Sophocles (he wrote a hundred and twenty-three).
It was Aeschylus, if Aristotle is to be believed, who came up with the
    innovation

of allowing the characters on stage to interact with one another, and not just
    with the chorus.
Somehow it seems so obvious in retrospect.

*

Is it too much to draw a connection with Lindsay Weir, the teenaged
    protagonist
of the wonderful *Freaks and Geeks*, canceled after a single season,
though it's one of the best things you've ever seen or will ever see on TV,

who, in the final episode, is loaned a copy of the Grateful Dead's nineteen-
     seventy
album, *American Beauty,* by a couple of Deadheads and who, after sixteen
and one-half episodes of the stress and perplexity and perpetual dis-
arrangement of being a teenager, finds, at last, true beauty,
and maybe, in just the same moment, finds also herself, dancing alone in her
     room
to the album's opening cut, the gorgeous and shimmering "Box of Rain"?

(And if it is too much then I will do it.
If it is just too much, we just must do it.)

Middle-aged fathers of America, let your daughters, let everyone's daughters,
     dance
alone in their rooms. Let them listen, if they want to listen, to the Grateful
     Dead.
Let them go secretly out onto the road, if they want, and follow the Grateful
     Dead,
or rather, whatever band it is now that moves teenagers to pile into vans
with their friends and hit the road after having lied to their blissfully gullible
parents and told them they were going off to "Math Camp" or to an
     "academic
summit." Let them get up to whatever it is they're going to get up to in
the dark, as the band plays its endless set, while they are still young enough
     to feel,
and even believe, that they will never die. Surely whatever the laws
of nature might be, among them must be the law that young people be
     allowed,
because they need to be allowed, and because they are, after all,
going to do it anyway, the freedom to do such things.

*

Did ancient Greek audiences sit in the dark? Did they get up to mischief?
Plato worried about the effects of drama on the Athenians, though I don't
     think

premature sexual activity among children was what he had in mind.

His famous image for human existence, and human delusion, was of a cave
in which we are chained, so that we can see only the shadows on the wall,
with the real world, the light that cast the shadows,

existing elsewhere, out of sight.
This, Plato said,
is our life.

*

This, Plato said, is our life. A shared dream of a life, an illusory life,
with reality taking place elsewhere. Hard not to notice how much the whole
    setup
resembles a movie theater, with us all facing in one direction, enjoying the
    illusion,

and somewhere behind us, the projector,
and somewhere beyond that,
the world.

THOUGH WE MAY AT TIMES
ADMIRE THE BEAUTY OF
THEIR WEAPONS

THESES TO BE NAILED TO THE DOOR OF THE
LAST OF THE GOLDEN AGE MOTION PICTURE
PALACES, FOLLOWING THE FINAL SCREENING

1. For every way of being assembled there is a way of being disassembled.

2. New songs for the new orchestras, new viruses for the new bodies.

3. For every new song a new way of hearing, a new way of failing to hear.

4. And where one speaks of "a way," one means, of course, countless ways. Many thousands of ways.

5. The pleasure of disassembly reveals itself as a compensation.

6. The song of decomposition is more bitter in the mouths of those who hear it than in the mouths of those who sing it.

7. Yet in the mouths of those who sing it, it could not be more bitter.

8. The world's task is perpetually to reassemble itself after having been decomposed by our acts of perception.

9. Which it pleases us by refusing to perform. Or merely pleases itself.

10. There is no pleasure in assembly, less in reassembly.

11. But assembly, though it compensates for nothing, makes certain pleasures possible.

12. If only in the imagination.

13. The disassembly of the imagination is its own kind of pleasure.

14. If only in the imagination.

15. And the decomposition of pleasure is its own kind of imagination.

16. If only in the remnants of disassembly. If only in the moments of gravid silence that precede the first moment of singing.

17. For every disorder there is an equal and opposite longing. We are commanded not to speak of it.

18. Not desiring to desire, desiring not to desire, not desiring to be desired, desiring not to be desired: these, at times, are the options available to us. But how to decide between them, without first deciding what one does not desire?

19. An ongoing process of disassembly in a manner that mimics assembly, that aspires from a certain vantage to be indistinguishable from assembly, is what we refer to as a style.

20. By *we* I mean those who inhabit the huts closest to mine.

21. The huts on this side of the river. The huts of those whose clothes are made of the same fibers as the clothes I put on in the morning.

22. When the light enters through the gaps where the wood has not been joined tightly to the wood.

23. A new way of failing to see, though the light is good. A new way of being unable to breathe.

24. Was being taught in the schools, causing discomfort among some of the older, less forward-thinking citizens.

25. The world is everything that is taught or goes untaught.

26. The world is everything that is erased.

27. The world is everything that is assembled or disassembled.

28. But that which decomposes in the tentative first light of morning occupies a category of its own.

SCREENSHOTS: *DELICATESSEN*

If the laws of physics
that seem to govern this universe
seem vaguely reminiscent

of those that apply in the world
of the Road Runner
and Wile E. Coyote,

we can surely attribute that,
in large part,
to the influence of vaudeville

both on the Looney
Tunes cartoons
and on tonight's special feature.

Vaudeville, perhaps,
along with a splash
of Kafka and Camus,

and a gesture toward
the parallel multiple lives
and dirty secrets

of the apartment building
from Hitchcock's *Rear Window*—
but here, no hint of the point of view

of the detached observer,
that reduces all
those lived-in rooms to a series

of display cases, as it were.
And what is left at the end,
when the clouds finally clear?

The hope that romance
can still be sweet
even when everything literally falls

apart; the time-honored truth
that revenge
is a dish that's best served not only cold

but sopping wet;
and the admission
that even those of us who, once upon

a time,
raised our fists in an angry group
while chanting *eat the rich!*, and who

still look forward to
the day when that fine
meal will at last be served, are for

the most part, for
the time being, generally
getting by in the only way

that this dark world permits,
which is to say,
turning our knives and forks

on one another.

SCREENSHOTS: *A SERIOUS MAN*

Mrs. Schrödinger: Erwin, dear, did you remember to feed the cat?
Erwin Schrödinger: Well, yes and no.

SCREENSHOTS: *CERTIFIED COPY*

While everyone else in the world is desperately
trying to state and stabilize
their identities, to, you know, *pin them down,*
like you'd do with the bodies of butterflies—

what a joy it is to watch these two
try on one after another role
as if they were tango-ing on a tilting,
decidedly unstable floor, to roll

and rock and shift from tempo to tempo
and, moment to moment, from style to style.
Why worry that you don't make a convincing
you, as long as, the whole while,

you can be somebody else? And that loss
of identity—who cares, if the man
sitting in your lap or in the passenger
seat, or the one you married, can

suddenly become a different person,
with no announcement, *in medias res?*
Need that concern you? O, irritable reaching
after reason, as Keats says,

go fuck yourself! Get thee away
from me! And just what has certainty
ever done for me anyway? Forget
all that, and come for a drive with me,

I have a surprise for you, and while
I'm at the wheel you can autograph
my copy. Perhaps you might make it out
to some rough production of tongue and breath,

some pattern of scrawl, some inkblot or other,
I might just yet decide to use
as a name or a sign of whatever it is
I am, or might, for my next trick, choose.

WANT

How do I want you? Let me count the ways.
I want you on demand. I want you streaming.
I want you half-asleep and in the taxi dreaming,
slouched and drifting in the back seat
in the June Manhattan haze.

I want you streaming. I want you on demand.
I want you in the back seats of a hundred thousand taxis.
I want you on every platform my device can access.
I want you arched and shivering
at the snap of my command.

I want you opening nationwide this week. I want you dreaming.
I hope you catch my meaning, dear. I want you on demand.
I want you in the taxi's headlights beaming bright. I want you
scheduled for inclusion
in my Pay Per Minute Plan.

I want you in the cab we hailed at twilight's last gleaming.
I want you on demand. So let us count the ways
I desire you to want me to want you to want me to want you.
I want you to understand
I could go on like this for days.

FIRE

1

How strange that it should have become
a metaphor for friendship:
We get along like a house on fire.
Though admittedly, the passions do burn,
and love can flare up
unexpected, uninvited,
can be kindled
by the spark of a delicate touch,
a smoldering glance, and,
once kindled, is difficult
to douse or discourage.
Perhaps this is wisdom,
to see that that
which we crave, to see
that that which makes
the long night bearable
and human life human
is that which consumes us,
the brisk, untamable
thing, prone to rage
like Achilles,
the thing that leaves
in its wake
the charred bitter remnants
of the houses that sheltered us
once, a blackened,
cremated terrain
of cinders, ashes,
and hollowed-out husks
that crumble

into powdery soot
when you take them
and rub them
between your fingers.

2

It is no cold fire,
that of the self-
incinerating stars,
no cosmic indifference,
though they lie too far
beyond us to warm us
and are best seen on nights
of deepest winter,
nights of insomnia,
when your sleepless, anxious
brain has your body
climb out of the bed
at three or four
in the morning, to walk
to the window and stand there,
looking out,
as if something out there
were speaking,
as if something
were speaking your name.

3

I was on fire, a person might say.
I was firing on all cylinders.
And what remains of them after? What walks
around in the bodies that once served as their vehicles?
The redwood, *Sequoia sempervirens,* grows

to such massive dimensions that the most intense forest
fire cannot slice its way through
to the core, even as its outer surface
is raging with flame. Leaving us to speculate
what it might be that inhabits that far center,
that has locked itself deep within, maintaining
a secret life, detached and indifferent,
which the flames of the world cannot touch.

4

"We are not only fighting hostile
armies,"
wrote William Tecumseh
Sherman, "but a hostile

people, and
must make old and young, rich and poor,
feel the hard hand
of war,

as well as their organized armies.
I know that this recent
movement
of mine through Georgia

has had a wonderful effect
in this respect."

5

This morning, having risen
early and walked
to the main cabin
through the dark, the path lit

by a handheld torch
that generates no heat,
I am reading
a recent opinion piece
in the *New York Times,*
whose author, in defense
of Sherman, points out that,
contrary to popular
impressions, the general's
forces did not reduce
all of Atlanta
to ash, but only
burned a mere half
of that city.

6

And Winston Churchill,
decades later,
justifying the fire-
bombing of the cities
of Germany, echoing
Sherman's language:
". . . the civilian population
around the target areas
must be made to feel
the weight of war."

7

And what is it in me (*do not move*
that prefers to think (*do not let the gods speak*
that to make people feel (*let the winds forgive*
is the task (*I have tried*
of the poet?

8

Small flames in metal cans kindled and maintained
by untouched, cold-skinned men, the private protected
flames of men who have only untouched
and cold-skinned friends, or no friends at all,
who are their own rough-built shelters, pitching
like poorly constructed ships on an unstable
sea, men holding their hands palms-down
over the lickings of flame. What is it
they are guarding, guarding by destroying? The small hopes
of men whose dreams are of dry interior
spaces, of warm laundered bedding, lit by
some invisible flame, a flame always present,
a flame never seen.

9

And you, you too have gotten the soot
of burning foreign cities
on your fingers, and have carried it though
passages, corridors, metal detectors,
houses of translators, houses of the soldiers
who carry out orders, houses of technicians
who design and program the targeting systems,
houses of physicians and metaphysicians,
houses of those who tend the public gardens,
houses long since abandoned, houses
built too close to the edge of the woods,
too close to the not-yet-properly-thinned-out
trees, constantly in danger of burning.

And the houses of those who have recorded,
in symbols and smudges, the acts and desires
of their people, the annals and chronicles, the tales,
that they might not be forgotten.

Pages inscribed to be read by the light
cast by the sun that sustains them.
Pages inscribed to be read by the light
cast by the fire that consumes them.

10

The fire and the wood are here,
Isaac said
to Abraham, his father.

But where is the lamb, father?
Where is the lamb for the burnt offering?

POSTSCRIPT TO *FIRE*

November 2018

The world will end in fire, not ice,
William Tecumseh Sherman said,
as we, horizons glowing red,
inhaled the ash of Paradise.

FIELD OF DEAD SUNFLOWERS

Something the gods have left behind,
something created to be disowned,
a place of purgation for wearied minds

where thoughts can be cleared of their sentiment,
hearts wrung roughly out like cheap sponges, a spot
a child might seek, having left behind

the walls and the windows it knows, to wander
and wring its songs free of their soapy sop.
Somewhere a flight of charred starlings might stop

and make landing, to perch like scarecrow-heads,
sun-scorched sentinels bored backwards by flight,
burnt free of the tiresome desire to soar

through celluloid-bright cerulean light.
Somewhere the disaster you make of your life
can be spoken through silence and, if understanding

requires more kindness than your gods can muster,
somewhere an approximation of peace
might settle on you like the grainy white powder

shat out of the back of a groaning crop-duster.

THE HOUSE COMMITTEE ON UN-AMERICAN ACTIVITIES PAUSES TO REFLECT ON ITS SERVICE TO THE COUNTRY

1. For the pleasure of administration is a kind of reassembly. A keeping things whole, a keeping things pure.

2. An idea of purity incipient in the writings of the founders themselves, even if they resisted it. Even if they had the good sense, at times, to feel a sense of discomfort that seeps into their writings.

3. Who goes to the movies anymore, anyway? To have to feel what everyone else is feeling.

4. Or, worse, to realize that what you feel is not what those around you are feeling.

5. Difficult to reconcile oneself to the knowledge that the scrapes and scratches and rough ratchetings, the blurs and burbles and the larking la-la-las and blathering bubbles that came swarming out of the mouth of the man in the marketplace stall was *speech*, that that unnatural, alien noise was language, just as much and not a penny less than those welcome, familiar sounds that lilt from your neighbors' mouths, from yours, like water from a spring, like a stream of silver coins from a jackpotting slot machine, like music.

6. Is that how it sounds to him? And how can he stand it if so, how can he bear it?

7. He must want to see you dead, silenced forever, you and all your kind exterminated in the name of a mad idea of hygiene there must be a word for in his language, a word you could not pronounce and would feel a bit sick if it forced itself on your ear.

8. And what if he tried to make you listen, what if he tried to make you understand?

9. Even his silence is strange, your silence can't sing to it or flow alongside it.

10. And did you say that life would be this, this constant living among strangers? Like Ruth, a human island in the alien corn. And if even corn can be alien to us, how much more so what is human, what is of our own flesh.

11. For language makes us anxious, when it does not get immediately to the *point*. We fear and dislike poets just as we fear and dislike people who come from foreign lands, for although, like us, they make noises with their mouths, we do not know what they mean.

12. Let no one, then, speak of brotherhood. Let this man, in particular, this foreigner, this poet, speak not of brotherhood, since you would not know it if he were to do so. He might just as well be speaking of the beauty of his weapons or the untraversable gulf between men.

13. Which you yourself do not believe in. Through the kindness of God there is in fact an untraversable gulf between men. We cannot, we need not, be brothers with those who occupy the huts across the river.

14. Though we may at times admire the beauty of their weapons.

15. We may even wish, perhaps, that we had made them ourselves, could carry them in our own hands.

16. Though you would never say this. For there is after all a place for feeling, and it is in the privacy of your own skull. Enhanced, where appropriate, by a large-screen TV and a high-quality streaming service.

17. Sitting alone in a darkened room, in the delicious autonomy of your feelings. What pleasure.

18. As, in the darkened meeting chambers, the Committee carries on ceaselessly through the night, continuing its work.

SING THE STRING
BENT SKYWARD

SPICES

You have gotten the scent of spices on your fingers
and carried it through customs, crossing borders
that isolate one people from another,
those who wear violet on Tuesday from those
who put on green on Thursday, those who bestow
the emphasis on the second syllable
from those who accentuate the third, the ones
who dust the meniscus of their evening coffee
with particles of cardamom from the people who,
in the way of their grandmothers and grandfathers,
show a preference for a sprinkling of cinnamon.

SCREENSHOTS: *PATERSON*

If poems are, as Ms. Moore once said,
imaginary gardens populated with real toads,

then what are we to make of this unreal world,
this imagined Garden State, that is studded with real poems?

SCREENSHOTS: *SYNECDOCHE, NEW YORK*

When you meet
the man
the man
you hired
to play you
hired to play "you"—

when you meet
the man
who's been hired
to play
the man
who was hired
to play you—

it isn't like looking
into a mirror—
one face seen, one constrained face
straining to be seen—

like a field
of dish antennae,
noses to the sky,
awaiting a message from home—

but it prompts the question,
just how good are *you*
in the role of you?
How convincing? How real?

Do people buy it,
the act, the day-in
day-out performance,
the ceaseless presentation

of self? Or do they see
through you, through to
the actor beneath,
the agent lurking

behind the screen,
the homunculus in
his cockpit, joystick
in hand, enjoying

the ride, inhabiting
the hell out of the role,
giving the performance
of his life?

SCREENSHOTS: *INSIDE LLEWYN DAVIS*

Because it is not the successful quest that fascinates—dragons defeated, villains
vanquished, cover-ups uncovered, the planet's perfect balance restored—
—or moralized tales of straining against the odds in the faith that genuine talent

and goodness of heart will eventually win out—no, not today—but the unfinished
task, the unfairly overlooked, the arrow gone astray. The under-
dog who stays under forever. Because, this time around, our sympathies lie

not with Bob Dylan, Nobel Laureate, but rather with the scruffy guy
who warmed up the crowd for him and then left, and now is getting beat up
in the alleyway out back, whose snow-trudging odyssey from New York to the Gates

of Horn, and back again, is the dark and unexperienced B-side of
A Star Is Born, or maybe *The Wizard of Oz,* the alternate ending the studios
sat on, a story to be repeated, never new, never old, and rarely acknowledged.

Not the driver that takes the Akron exit, but the one who is too afraid to,
who almost does and then doesn't, who sticks to the path and just drives on into the dark.
Not Ulysses, but some unnamed alley cat abandoned somewhere outside of Chicago.

Not Llewyn's voice, as much as it moves us, no, but the unheard harmony part
sung by the singer who made his exit before the first light flickered up to the screen,
before the first note was sounded, who, for silent reasons of his own, jumped from

the wrong bridge, to wander the immaterial streets and to play the old
    songs and haunt
the footnotes of the history of some unsuspected invisible republic.
    Or, alternatively,
the unwritten, unread, heretofore unfilmed alternative history of this
    one.

SONG TO BE SUNG WHEN THE INSTRUMENTS FALTER

So he sat down and wrote a poem about egrets
and how they reminded him of thoughts too pure
for us, too pregnant with the awful dignity
of disaster, and then
he took the egrets out,
and he walked around with that image weighing him down
like a sack of wet grain in his stomach, so that he swayed
like a man who was slightly drunk, who was remembering,
perhaps, or perhaps simply forgetting to forget
the early days of some love affair or other,
making slow, sculptural gestures as an actor would,
but an actor with no audience, a gladiator
in an empty arena, waiting, as the echoes
of the jeers and applause of thousands ascend
like newly freed souls and evaporate into
the empty void that sheaths the planet. Left
outside, exposed to the elements, anger
will not be transformed into love, but the cordlike
green tendrils that sprout out of it will linger
for a while in the heavy and darkening evening
air, like voices just on the other side
of an open door, the way they carry in the evening,
out over the flat surface water of a lake,
and your name is someone else's name, someone
you were forced to abandon, someone you knew once, and loved.

SCORDATURA

Sing the string
bent skyward,
sing the string
tuned low
toward the floor.
The cheap
black plastic
radio tuned
to a station defunct
for a decade
or more.
Broadcasting from
a secluded spot
eight hundred miles
from town, that was
your childhood,
straining, off-balance,
leaning forward
into the void
to hear those isolate
patches of meaningful
sound, those sonic
stragglers struggling
to pierce
the white noise
the ether-screen
like dolphins
trying to break
the surface.
The unendorsed word
borrowed from Farsi
borrowed from Finnish
borrowed from French

that burrows its way
into conversation
at the precise point
to elicit that illicit
smile, that sign of
unacknowledged
longing
officials can neither
confirm nor deny.
The unidentified
substances brought
by camel train
or container ship
from the frayed and
time-darkened
edges of the
atlas that's passed
for ten thousand
nights from hand
to antique hand,
mixed into the pigments,
mixed into the spices,
mixed into the blood.
The unprogrammed twist
of the elbow
or ankle
thrown into the wrestle
or dance at an
opportune
moment, so that
your opponent
or partner
discovers herself
surprised and helplessly
prone on the floor,
the audience finding

itself on its feet
applauding, awash
with sudden astonished
wonder. The alien
coin slipped into
the currency stream
to be swapped for an hour
of pleasure,
the foreign
delights slipped
into the ceaseless barrage
of unsanctioned
satisfactions.
The unimproved road
that carries you
to the unapproved
destination.
The intangible sadness
of the inscrutable faces
of the children whose
discordant laments
greet you there.

THE NIGHTINGALE

("Le rossignol," Paul Verlaine, 1866)

All my memories, turbulent birds, wildly flying,
Collapse and converge on me, shrieking and crying,
Falling and settling in the yellow foliage,
Where the crooked alderwood mirror-image
Of my heart floats in the silver-violet Water
Of Regrets, and melancholy flows nearby.
Then, after they fall, ominous noises,
Appeased by a humid breeze as it rises,
Expanding bit by bit through the branches, so soothing
That before you know it you hear nothing.
Nothing but the voice that celebrates the absent one.
Nothing but the voice—so languid!—of the song-
Bird that was, so many years ago, my First Love,
And who sings, even now, like it's the first day of
Its being, and the world's. And in the sad splendor
Of the moon as it rises, pale and solemn, in this tender
And melancholy night, sagging with the heaviness
Of summer, and of silence, of things we cannot guess,
Rocked gently on the azure by the wind's caress,
The trembling tree, the nightingale's mournful address.

THE ADVENTURE

There will never be a complete catalog of varieties
of human happiness, human desire, or human cruelty.
Of happiness, we can say that it is by its nature
unrepeatable. The thrill is that it happens only once.
A performance, like the first taste of chocolate or
a first kiss, cannot be preserved or repeated.
At most we can hope for certain evidence
that the event occurred: photographs, recordings, rumors,
recollections that fade and grow steadily less
reliable with each passing year, none of which
come at all close to replicating the experience
of really being there. The movies, though, are timeless:
no viewing is privileged, no viewing comes closer
than any other viewing to being a genuinely
'true' or 'real' experience (whatever, in this context,
true or *real* might mean), and there is therefore
no way to attach to a film a precise date
and time. There is only the time when *you* saw it,
and how it moved you then, how it changed you. Yet films are,
if anything, even more poignant in the way
they remind us of what has been lost and what we cannot
recover, if only because the illusion
is that they bring us so much closer to it
in the act of watching, and because that illusion
persists so much longer. Repeatable? Sure.
But the actors have all passed away, or eventually
will; the objects, if they were real to begin with,
have all been destroyed, or at some point they will be;
the very landscapes and places in which
the characters are placed and carry on their affairs
have, if they weren't simply constructed sets
from the start, been altered by the passage of time,
most likely not for the better, in the years

since the film crew planted their camera and captured
their footage. The alluring sadness, for instance,
visible in the eyes of Lea Massari
in Antonioni's *L'Avventura*
in the scenes that take place just before she disappears—
she is feeling a distance from her lover, Sandro,
for reasons we, the viewers, can sense but can't quite
get inside, and which we find all the more compelling
for our very failure to quite get inside them—
reminds us that that world, that Italy, that cinematic
moment, have vanished; even though it is there,
in front of our eyes, larger, as we sometimes say,
than life, it is in fact as finally and irrevocably
gone as is Massari's character, Anna,
who disappears from the film without explanation.
Which brings us back to cruelty. It is perhaps
the cruelty of the world, or perhaps just the cruelty
of art, which depicts and pretends to preserve
the world, to keep this vanishing constantly in view,
while at the same time giving us the illusion
that it can be avoided, defeated, overcome,
each image returned to without limitation,
resurrected any number of times for our own
reassurance and enjoyment, the film replayed
and replayed, the PAUSE button always at the ready
if we want to contemplate, at our leisure, the barren,
virtually inhuman landscapes, or Sandro's magnificent
indifference, or Monica Vitti's face,
which always reminds me a little of the face
of the first woman I made love to, which happened
around the time I first saw *L'Avventura,*
that first viewing still the most profound, the most shocking,
as if I had discovered a new and unanticipated
version of myself. I suppose the fantasy
is that no one ever needs to die,
that everything that happens survives somewhere,

if not as an object then as an image
or a thought, a strip of celluloid, or a matrix
of digitized information on a hard drive
stored in an underground vault underneath
the deserts of New Mexico. Or, if not that,
then in the sentimental fragmentary conversations
of people who, for as long as they can manage,
until advancing time gets the better of them,
gather to relive and recollect their chosen slices
of the past. After that first time, I walked home
and, as I recall, the moon was full. What was it
I'd located in myself? An unrecognized capacity
for greed? For brutal passion? I had always
desired the pleasures life offered, but in
moderation; now I wanted them excessively, I wanted
life itself, and also my desire for it, to be
excessive, as if—it was a ten-minute walk
back to my parents' house, and because the night
was frigid, the air was clear like music, Chopin
or Satie, precise and faraway, and the stars
were tiny distant torches looking down—as if
I'd be protected if I made myself someone whose desire
refused to concede any limit, as if I
could be safe and free and live forever if only
I could empty myself, leaving nothing but an ache
that ached to be filled, to be resolved, to find a way to be
pure hunger, absolute. To be nothing but hunger.

ODYSSEUS DEPARTING

Sometime between the seventh day
and the seventy-seventh, or maybe the seven
hundred and seventy-seventh, when the Maker's
task was, more or less, completed
and all that remained was to tidy up
some debris and perform the final inspections,
Odysseus, his journeys and homecomings
lying still in his future, not yet the stuff
of myth or of legend, not yet a set
of tales to be told round the fire, not yet
a make-work project for generations
of scholars and interpreters, finished supper
and announced that he would go to bed early.
He was to depart in the morning. Lying
in that massive oak-rooted bed, the soft body
of Penelope prone beside him, he watched
the last light fade to blackness, turning his wife
from a three-dimensional figure into
a *film noir* silhouette. She was worried
about Telemachus growing up without a father,
and so he stroked her hair and gently
reassured her: *The boy will never be without
a father, even when his father is far
away*. He did not say, because
he knew she would hear it whether he said it
or not, and that it would be better
if he did not say it, *And even when your husband
is far away, you will never be without
a husband*. Neither of them had any idea
how long he would be gone, neither knew
of the plague of suitors that was poised to descend
on the house, nor had she yet begun

the skein-raveling and skein-unraveling
that would occupy her hands, and hold them at bay,
for years. Odysseus could never really sleep
on nights like this, the night prior to a journey,
but he did not dread the long hours of in-
between-ness, the dim light like being underwater,
his body pressed against her warm and cherished body.
The weight of the years to come, of the battles
and travels, dimly sensed, weighed down on him,
and although he had meant what he said, and all
that she had heard even though he had not said it,
he was a human and so not immune
to fear, to dread, to prospective regret
projected toward every night that his wife
would be forced to sleep the great bed alone,
growing older by the hour, his son
growing older by the hour, while he laid
his body down who could say where, on cold rocks,
most likely, under unrecognized stars,
wherever a space could be found, between bodies
or in the space where there were no bodies,
aching for her presence. His body frisked
by the waters and winds. He was not afraid
of dying—he almost craved to know
how it felt, that last journey, that adventure—
but the idea of staying dead, forever,
separated from wife and son, was awful.
Our fear of death, he thought, *inclines us
to certain theories regarding time
and the gods.* In the morning, he sat at the table
with her, for an hour, almost, saying nothing,
sipping tea, and when it came time to go,
she kissed him gently on the cheek, then on the lips,
harder. Then they went outside
to stand in the sun, and she lifted up their boy
so the father could look back and see them both

when he reached the edge of the property,
which he did, then turned away, and shouldered
his pack, with the lunch she'd prepared for him,
and marched down that as yet untranslated road.

Acknowledgments

I owe gratitude and debts of various sorts to Robert Hass, Brenda Hillman, Forrest Gander, Sharon Olds, Brett Hall Jones, and all at the Community of Writers; to Tim Tomlinson, Ravi Shankar, and everyone at the New York Writers Workshop in Sardinia; to Meryl Natchez and Larry Rafferty, and to H. L. Hix.

And to Heather: gratitude, yes, and admiration, amazement, wonder, and all my love.

Publication Credits

Poems in this manuscript have been previously published, or are in some cases forthcoming, as follows:

The American Journal of Poetry: Field of Dead Sunflowers
                                     Fire
                                     Silence and Residue of Waters

Bennington Review: That Life

Copper Nickel: Marvelous Things Without Number

Cortland Review: Poem for Gord Downie

Forklift, Ohio: Andre Gregory Said

The Laurel Review: American Beauty

Miramar: The Poem You Will Not Live to Write

Narrative Magazine: At Limantour
                                     Free Huey P. Newton with Every
                                         Purchase
                                     Next Life
                                     Scordatura

Nostos: Screenshots: *Certified Copy*
                                     Screenshots: *Inside Llewyn Davis*

Plume: Screenshots: *Being John Malkovich*
                                     Screenshots: *Eternal Sunshine of the
                                         Spotless Mind*
                                     Screenshots: *No Country for Old Men*
                                     Self-Portrait in Invisible Ink
                                     Screenshots: *Synecdoche, New York*

A Smartish Pace:	The House Committee on Un-American Activities. . .
Subtropics:	The Adventure Landscape with Ambiguous Symbols
Zyzzyva:	The Garden of Earthly Delights Zapruder Film Blooper Reel

"At Limantour," "Free Huey P. Newton with Every Purchase," "Next Life," and "Scordatura" were awarded second place in the Ninth Annual Narrative Magazine Poetry Contest in 2016.

Versions of "Muse," "At Limantour," "The Poem You Will Not Live to Write," and "Song to Be Sung When the Instruments Falter," translated into Greek by Lena Kallergi, appeared in *Poetix* (Athens, 2020).

"Marvelous Things Without Number" was republished on Verse Daily, May 27, 2020.

"The Poem You Will Not Live to Write" was republished in *Why to These Rocks: 50 Years of Poetry from the Community of Writers* (Heyday Books).

"The Garden of Earthly Delights" was republished in *Best American Poetry 2020.*

Princeton Series of Contemporary Poets